WORK

WORK

Life Application® Bible Studies ™

Valerie Weidemann
James C. Galvin, Ed.D.

Tyndale House Publishers, Inc.
Wheaton, Illinois

Life Application Bible Studies: *Work* copyright © 1996 by Tyndale House Publishers, Inc., Wheaton, Illinois 60189. All rights reserved.

Cover illustration copyright © 1996 by José Ortega

Developed exclusively for Tyndale House Publishers by The Livingstone Corporation. Bruce B. Barton, David R. Veerman, Daryl J. Lucas, Michael Kendrick, Christopher D. Hudson, James C. Galvin, Valerie Weidemann, project staff.

Life Application notes are adapted from the *Life Application Bible,* © 1988, 1989, 1990, 1991 by Tyndale House Publishers, Inc.

Life Application is a registered trademark of Tyndale House Publishers, Inc.

Life Application Bible Studies is a trademark of Tyndale House Publishers, Inc.

Scripture quotations marked KJV are taken from the *Holy Bible,* King James Version.

Scripture quotations marked NIV are taken from the *Holy Bible,* New International Version®. Copyright © 1973, 1978, 1984 by International Bible Society. Used by permission of Zondervan Publishing House. All rights reserved. The "NIV" and "New International Version" trademarks are registered in the United States Patent and Trademark Office by International Bible Society. Use of either trademark requires permission of International Bible Society.

Scripture quotations marked NLT are taken from the *Holy Bible,* New Living Translation, copyright © 1996. Used by permission of Tyndale House Publishers, Inc., Wheaton, Illinois 60189. All rights reserved. *New Living Translation* is a trademark of Tyndale House Publishers, Inc.

ISBN 0-8423-0159-3

Printed in the United States of America

00	99	98	97	96			
8	7	6	5	4	3	2	1

Contents

A Note to Bible Study Leaders   *vii*

LESSON ONE
A Job Made in Heaven   *1*

LESSON TWO
Work Is Hard Work   *11*

LESSON THREE
Life Begins on Friday   *19*

LESSON FOUR
You Deserve a Break   *27*

LESSON FIVE
You Cannot Do It All   *35*

LESSON SIX
If It Were Not for My Boss   *45*

A Note to Bible Study Leaders

Trying to use something that does not work often brings frustration and disappointment. On the other hand, using something that works well is a delight. The Life Application Bible Studies are the latter, especially if you want to help the people in your small group apply the Bible to their lives. That is because these are the most application-oriented Bible study guides available, covering a variety of topics to meet a range of interests and needs.

WHAT IS APPLICATION

The best way to define application is to first determine what it is *not*. Application is *not* just accumulating knowledge. This helps us discover and understand facts and concepts, but it stops there. History is filled with philosophers who knew what the Bible said but failed to apply it to their lives, keeping them from believing and changing. Many think that understanding is the goal of Bible study, but it is really only the beginning.

Application is *not* illustration. Illustration only tells us how someone else handled a similar situation. While we may empathize with that person, we still have little direction for our personal situation.

Application is *not* just making a passage "relevant." Making the Bible relevant only helps us to see that the same lessons that were true in Bible times are true today; it does not show us how to apply them to the problems and pressures of our individual lives.

What, then, is application? Application begins by knowing and understanding God's Word and its timeless truths. *But we cannot stop there.* If we do, God's Word may not change our life, and studying the Bible may become dull, difficult, tedious, and tiring. A good application focuses on the truth of God's Word, shows the reader what to do about what is being read, and motivates the reader to respond to what God is teaching. All three are essential to application.

A NOTE TO BIBLE STUDY LEADERS viii

Application is putting into practice what we already know (see Mark 4:24 and Hebrews 5:14) and answering the question "So what?" by confronting us with the right questions and motivating us to take action (see 1 John 2:5-6 and James 2:26). Application is deeply personal—unique for each individual. It is making a relevant truth a personal truth and involves developing a strategy and action plan to live your life in harmony with the Bible. It is the biblical "how to" of life.

This is what the Life Application Bible Studies were designed to do—to make relevant truth personal and to help you live your life in harmony with the Bible.

ABOUT THIS STUDY GUIDE

Each Life Application Bible Study is made up of six lessons. The lessons are divided into four easy-to-lead sections. The first section, entitled "Starter," contains two interesting questions that will get your group talking. It also introduces your group to the area of life covered by the lesson.

The second section, entitled "Study," contains three sets of verses, notes, and questions. The verses appear in three different translations of the Bible— King James Version (KJV), New International Version (NIV), and New Living Translation (NLT). You can select the translation you and your group prefer or read all three comparatively. The notes summarize the point of the passage quickly and help your group see how the passage applies to their lives. The questions help your group examine God's view on the topic as well as their own views. In addition, the questions help your group members think about practical steps they can take to apply God's Word to their lives.

The third section, entitled "Summary," reviews the important points in each lesson and calls the participants to action.

The fourth section, entitled "Supplemental Questions," gives you additional Bible passages, notes, and questions to extend the lesson or to replace some of the passages from the "Study" section.

USING THIS STUDY GUIDE

Begin each lesson with prayer, asking the Holy Spirit for guidance through and wisdom for your study. Then begin the study, working your way through the

Starter, Study, and Summary sections of the lesson. Here are the recommended time allotments for each section of a lesson based on a sixty- or ninety-minute study:

Section	60-Minute Study	90-Minute Study
Starter:	5 minutes	10 minutes
Study: first passage	15 minutes	20 minutes
Study: second passage	15 minutes	20 minutes
Study: third passage	15 minutes	20 minutes
Summary	10 minutes	20 minutes

The time allotments are only suggestions. Larger groups may require more time for discussion. Also, some groups may be more talkative than others, so the time required to complete the studies will vary from group to group. When you have finished the lesson, end your study with prayer.

ADAPTING THIS STUDY GUIDE

The Life Application Bible Studies have been designed for groups to work through in six weeks, but they can easily be adapted to extend the study to twelve weeks. Here are some alternatives for extending the study:

LENGTH	SECTIONS
12 **weeks (slower)**	Work through the Starter section and one or two passages from the Study section the first week. Then work through the last passage from the Study section and the Summary section for the next week.
12 **weeks (deeper)**	Work through the Starter and Study sections the first week. Then select three supplemental passages from the Supplemental Questions section and work through these passages as well as the Summary section for the next week.

THE GOAL OF THIS STUDY GUIDE

No note, by itself, can apply Scripture directly to your life. It can only teach, direct, inspire, recommend, and urge. It can give you the resources and direction you need to apply the Bible. But only *you* can take these resources and put them into practice. James said it clearly:

> *Do not merely listen to the word, and so deceive yourselves. Do what it says. Anyone who listens to the word but does not do what it says is like a man who looks at his face in a mirror and, after looking at himself, goes away and immediately forgets what he looks like. But the man who looks intently into the perfect law that gives freedom, and continues to do this, not forgetting what he has heard, but doing it—he will be blessed in what he does.*

James 1:22-25, NIV

**LESSON
ONE**

A Job Made in Heaven

You do not have to have a perfect job to serve God! Although God does bless some people with wonderful careers, he does not promise us a job made in heaven. This lesson will teach you God's purpose for work and how to honor him, even in what the world considers to be an ordinary job. You will be encouraged to use the abilities God has given you in the job where he has placed you.

STARTER

1. *When you were little, what did you want to be when you grew up?*

2. *What is the best job you have ever had?*

LESSON 1

◆◆◆◆◆◆◆ *STUDY*

Read the following three sets of Bible passages and application notes.
Answer the questions for each set before moving on to the next.

Genesis 3:17-19

KJV

And unto Adam he said, Because thou hast hearkened unto the voice of thy wife, and hast eaten of the tree, of which I commanded thee, saying, Thou shalt not eat of it: cursed is the ground for thy sake; in sorrow shalt thou eat of it all the days of thy life; Thorns also and thistles shall it bring forth to thee; and thou shalt eat the herb of the field; In the sweat of thy face shalt thou eat bread, till thou return unto the ground; for out of it wast thou taken: for dust thou art, and unto dust shalt thou return.

NIV

To Adam he said, "Because you listened to your wife and ate from the tree about which I commanded you, 'You must not eat of it,' Cursed is the ground because of you; through painful toil you will eat of it all the days of your life. It will produce thorns and thistles for you, and you will eat the plants of the field. By the sweat of your brow you will eat your food until you return to the ground, since from it you were taken; for dust you are and to dust you will return."

NLT

And to Adam he said, "Because you listened to your wife and ate the fruit I told you not to eat, I have placed a curse on the ground. All your life you will struggle to scratch a living from it. It will grow thorns and thistles for you, though you will eat of its grains. All your life you will sweat to produce food, until your dying day. Then you will return to the ground from which you came. For you were made from dust, and to the dust you will return."

Work is God's idea. After God created Adam, he placed Adam in charge of caring for the Garden of Eden. The work was enjoyable and completely fulfilling. But when Adam and Eve sinned, they were kicked out of Eden, and their work became a struggle against the elements in order to provide food, clothing, and shelter for themselves and their family. Work was no longer refreshing and delightful but a curse, involving painful toil. Today, we are still under this curse, but it is possible to experience moments of satisfaction in our work. If we are searching for the perfect job, however, we will only be disappointed. Every job will involve frustration and toil. But we should strive to do our best and honor God in our work.

3. Why do you think so many people are unfulfilled or dissatisfied in their jobs?

4. Why is it important to realize that work is created by God but spoiled by sin?

5. What struggles or challenges do you face at work?

6. How does this passage enable you to face those difficulties?

LESSON 1

Matthew 25:14-15, 19-21

KJV

For the kingdom of heaven is as a man travelling into a far country, who called his own servants, and delivered unto them his goods . . . and straightway took his journey. . . . After a long time the lord of those servants cometh, and reckoneth with them. And so he that had received five talents came and brought other five talents, saying, Lord, thou deliveredst unto me five talents: behold, I have gained beside them five talents more. His lord said unto him, Well done, thou good and faithful servant: thou hast been faithful over a few things, I will make thee ruler over many things: enter thou into the joy of thy lord.

NIV

Again, it will be like a man going on a journey, who called his servants and entrusted his property to them. . . . Then he went on his journey. . . . After a long time the master of those servants returned and settled accounts with them. The man who had received the five talents brought the other five. "Master," he said, "you entrusted me with five talents. See, I have gained five more." His master replied, "Well done, good and faithful servant! You have been faithful with a few things; I will put you in charge of many things. Come and share your master's happiness!"

NLT

Again, the Kingdom of Heaven can be illustrated by the story of a man going on a trip. He called together his servants and gave them money to invest for him while he was gone . . . and then left on his trip. After a long time their master returned from his trip and called them to give an account of how they had used his money. The servant to whom he had entrusted the five bags of gold said, "Sir, you gave me five bags of gold to invest and I have doubled the amount." The master was full of praise. "Well done, my good and faithful servant. You have been faithful in handling this small amount, so now I will give you many more responsibilities. Let's celebrate together!"

Jesus is coming back—we know that is true. Does this mean we should quit our jobs in order to serve God? No, it means we are to use what we have well until he returns. The talents in this parable represent any kind of resource we are given. God gives us time, gifts, money, and other resources according to our abilities. He expects us to use them wisely. For a few people, this may mean changing professions. For most of us, it means doing our daily work out of love for God. You are responsible to use well the talents God has given you.

5   LESSON 1

7. *When have you been tempted to quit your job? Why?*

8. *What is one skill or talent that God has given you?*

9. *How does that skill help you fulfill your responsibilities at work?*

10. *How can you make better use of the talents God has given you?*

---

1 Corinthians 7:20-22

KJV

Let every man abide in the same calling wherein he was called. Art thou called being a servant? care not for it: but if thou mayest be made free, use it rather. For he that is called in the Lord, being a servant, is the Lord's freeman: likewise also he that is called, being free, is Christ's servant.

NIV

Each one should remain in the situation which he was in when God called him. Were you a slave when you were called? Don't let it trouble you—although if you can gain your freedom, do so. For he who was a slave when he was called by the Lord is the Lord's freedman; similarly, he who was a free man when he was called is Christ's slave.

NLT

You should continue on as you were when God called you. Are you a slave? Don't let that worry you—but if you get a chance to be free, take it. And remember, if you were a slave when the Lord called you, the Lord has now set you free from the awful power of sin. And if you were free when the Lord called you, you are now a slave of Christ.

LESSON 1

6

Apparently the Corinthians were making sweeping changes without thinking through the ramifications. Paul wrote to say that people should be Christians where God has placed them. You can do God's work and demonstrate your faith anywhere. Often we are so concerned about what we could be doing for God elsewhere that we miss great opportunities right here and now. Paul says that when someone becomes a Christian, he or she should usually continue with the work he or she has previously been doing—provided it isn't immoral or unethical. Don't assume that you are in the wrong line of work. You may be just exactly where God wants you.

11. In what way can your work also be a ministry?

12. How can you know if your job is the one that God wants you to have?

13. What commonsense advice would you give to a new believer who finds him- or herself in the wrong line of work?

14. How can you ensure that you are doing your work for God's glory?

◆◆◆◆◆◆◆ **SUMMARY**

Scripture does not tell us how to find the "perfect" job, but it does tell us that no job is perfect anymore. Work was created by God but spoiled by the Fall. God gives us work to do and asks us to do it for his glory. We

LESSON 1

should carefully explore the gifts God has given us and find work to match those gifts and then commit ourselves to faithfully complete our work.

15. *What could you do differently this week that would bring honor to God through your work?*

◆◆◆◆ SUPPLEMENTAL QUESTIONS

Read Exodus 35:30–36:7.

This passage describes the blending of various artistic and construction skills in the building of the traveling sanctuary. It is easy to think that God would provide people with "spiritual" abilities like leadership, preaching, and healing to serve in the tabernacle. And yet Bezalel was filled with God's Spirit in such a way that all his artistic and design skills took on an added quality appropriate to the work he was called to do. God is the source of our skills, and he wants us to use them. Even if our work is not what we think of as "spiritual," it can still be done to God's glory.

16. *Why do we tend to think that only spiritual work is worthwhile?*

17. *What do you do well that some or many would not consider spiritual?*

18. *How can you change the way you work to better employ the creative abilities God has given you?*

Read 2 Samuel 5:12.

Although the pagan kingdoms based their greatness on conquest, power, and wealth, David knew that his greatness came only from God. He kept his ambition under control by keeping a

LESSON 1

close relationship with God. Although he was famous, successful, and well liked, David gave God first place in his life and served the people according to God's purposes.

19. How can ambition keep us from serving God in our work?

20. How can we keep our ambition under control?

21. What can you do at work to acknowledge God and fulfill his purposes?

Read Isaiah 45:1.

> *This is the only place in the Bible where a Gentile ruler is said to be "anointed." God anointed Cyrus because he had a special task for him to do for Israel. Cyrus allowed God's city, Jerusalem, to be rebuilt, and he set the exiles free to resettle there. Few kings of Israel or Judah did as much for God's people as Cyrus did.*

22. What does it mean to be anointed by God for a special task?

23. How does God call us to work for him today?

24. What can Christians do if they feel they have missed God's calling for their life?

Read John 3:22-30.

John's main purpose was to point people to Christ. His disciples wondered why he continued to baptize people even after Jesus came onto the scene. John explained that because God had given him his work, he had to continue it until God called him to do something else. Even with Jesus beginning his own ministry, John could still do the job God had given him.

25. What does John's response to his disciples reveal about his attitude toward work?

26. Is it easy or difficult for you to stay humble in your line of work? What helps you to stay humble?

27. How can we keep from becoming distracted or sidetracked from the work God gives us?

Read 1 Corinthians 15:58.

Paul says that because of the Resurrection, nothing we do is in vain. Sometimes we hesitate to commit ourselves fully to our work because we do not see any results. But if we maintain a heavenly perspective, we will not expect to always see the good that results from our efforts. Do not let discouragement over an apparent lack of results keep you from working hard. Do the good that you have the opportunity to do, knowing that your work will have eternal results. Be confident that when you work for God, all your effort is worthwhile.

28. What kind of work is never a waste of time?

LESSON 1   10

29. *In light of this passage, how can we deal with discouragement on the job?*

30. *How can you remind yourself of this passage the next time you feel discouraged about your work?*

LESSON TWO

Work Is Hard Work

When we are doing work that we are good at and enjoy doing, work can be fun! But because of the Fall, even good jobs involve difficult or boring tasks. The Bible does not promise us that work will be easy, rewarding, or personally fulfilling. In fact, if we try to find meaning in life from our work rather than from God, we will never be satisfied. This lesson will teach you that God, not your job, is the source of ultimate joy and that any pleasure you do receive from your work is a gift from him.

◆◆◆◆◆ *STARTER*

1. *What is the hardest job you have ever had?*

2. *What aspect of your current or most recent job do you find boring?*

L E S S O N 2   12

◆◆◆◆◆◆◆ *STUDY*

Read the following three sets of Bible passages and application notes. Answer the questions for each set before moving on to the next.

Ecclesiastes 2:17-19

KJV	NIV	NLT
Therefore I hated life; because the work that is wrought under the sun is grievous unto me: for all is vanity and vexation of spirit. Yea, I hated all my labour which I had taken under the sun: because I should leave it unto the man that shall be after me. And who knoweth whether he shall be a wise man or a fool? yet shall he have rule over all my labour wherein I have laboured, and wherein I have shewed myself wise under the sun. This is also vanity.	So I hated life, because the work that is done under the sun was grievous to me. All of it is meaningless, a chasing after the wind. I hated all the things I had toiled for under the sun, because I must leave them to the one who comes after me. And who knows whether he will be a wise man or a fool? Yet he will have control over all the work into which I have poured my effort and skill under the sun. This too is meaningless.	So now I hate life because everything done here under the sun is so irrational. Everything is meaningless, like chasing the wind. I am disgusted that I must leave the fruits of my hard work to others. And who can tell whether my successors will be wise or foolish? And yet they will control everything I have gained by my skill and hard work. How meaningless!

As the writer of Ecclesiastes looked back over everything he had done, most of it seemed meaningless to him. One of the truths he realized was that hard work done solely to earn money and gain possessions bears no lasting fruit. That is not to say that hard work done with proper motives is wrong. We must work to survive, and we are responsible for the physical needs of those under our care. But the reward of hard work done to glorify ourselves will be passed on to those who may later lose or spoil it. Such self-centered toil often leads to grief, while serving God leads to everlasting joy.

3. *What incentives or rewards seem to motivate people to work hard?*

4. *How can we determine whether we are working for the right reasons?*

5. *When you ultimately look back on your life, do you think you will be happy with your accomplishments? Why or why not?*

6. *How can we avoid the sense of futility and frustration that the writer of Ecclesiastes faced at the end of his life?*

Ecclesiastes 2:24-26

KJV

There is nothing better for a man, than that he should eat and drink, and that he should make his soul enjoy good in his labour. This also I saw, that it was from the hand of God. For who can eat, or who else can hasten hereunto, more than I? For God giveth to a man that is good in his sight wisdom, and knowledge, and joy: but to the sinner he giveth travail, to gather and to heap up, that he may give to him that is good before God. This also is vanity and vexation of spirit.

NIV

A man can do nothing better than to eat and drink and find satisfaction in his work. This too, I see, is from the hand of God, for without him, who can eat or find enjoyment? To the man who pleases him, God gives wisdom, knowledge and happiness, but to the sinner he gives the task of gathering and storing up wealth to hand it over to the one who pleases God. This too is meaningless, a chasing after the wind.

NLT

So I decided there is nothing better than to enjoy food and drink and to find satisfaction in work. Then I realized that this pleasure is from the hand of God. For who can eat or enjoy anything apart from him? God gives wisdom, knowledge, and joy to those who please him. But if a sinner becomes wealthy, God takes the wealth away and gives it to those who please him. Even this, however, is meaningless, like chasing the wind.

LESSON 2   14

Is the writer recommending that we make life a big, irresponsible party? No, he is encouraging us to take pleasure in what we are doing now and to enjoy work because it comes from God's hand. Those who really know how to enjoy their work are those who see their responsibilities as a gift from God, thank him for their work, and serve him through it. Those without God have no relief from toil and no direction to guide them through the struggles of life.

7. According to Ecclesiastes, whose work does God bless? Whose work is a futile endeavor?

8. How can an unsatisfied person find the satisfaction that comes from the hand of God?

9. What keeps us from finding satisfaction in our work?

10. How can we more effectively pray for and about our work?

Ecclesiastes 5:18-19

KJV

Behold that which I have seen: it is good and comely for one to eat and to drink, and to enjoy the good of all his labour that he taketh under the sun all the days of his life, which God giveth him: for it is his portion. Every man also to whom God hath given riches and wealth, and hath given him power to eat thereof, and to take his portion, and to rejoice in his labour; this is the gift of God.

NIV

Then I realized that it is good and proper for a man to eat and drink, and to find satisfaction in his toilsome labor under the sun during the few days of life God has given him— for this is his lot. Moreover, when God gives any man wealth and possessions, and enables him to enjoy them, to accept his lot and be happy in his work—this is a gift of God.

NLT

Even so, I have noticed one thing, at least, that is good. It is good for people to eat well, drink a good glass of wine, and enjoy their work—whatever they do under the sun—for however long God lets them live. And it is a good thing to receive wealth from God and the good health to enjoy it. To enjoy your work and accept your lot in life—that is indeed a gift from God.

Your ability to find satisfaction in your work depends to a large extent upon your attitude. You will become dissatisfied if you lose the sense of purpose God intended for your work. But you can enjoy work if you remember that it is created and given to you by God, realize that the fruit of your labor is a gift from God's hand, and view your work as a way to serve God. Most important, remember that true happiness is not found in your accomplishments or ability to accumulate but in your relationship with God.

11. *What factors do people usually consider when applying for or accepting a new job?*

12. *Why do many people choose higher-paying positions over jobs they really enjoy?*

LESSON 2   16

13. *How can unrealistic expectations take the joy out of work?*

14. *How can you ensure that your expectations for your job are realistic?*

◆◆◆◆◆◆◆ SUMMARY

These passages from Ecclesiastes encourage us to enjoy our work but discourage us from looking to our own accomplishments for meaning and purpose in life. Without God, there is no lasting reward or benefit in hard work! Work done with the wrong attitude will leave us empty, but work accepted as an assignment from God can bring joy. Accept the work God gives you as a gift from him, and determine to do it cheerfully.

15. *In what ways do you need to adjust your attitude toward your work or your expectations of what you will get from it?*

◆◆◆◆◆◆◆ SUPPLEMENTAL QUESTIONS

Read Ruth 2:1-13.

Ruth's task, though menial and tiring, was done faithfully. We are often asked to do jobs that do not require our full potential. The work God gives you may be all you can do right now, or it may be the work God wants you to do. Or, as in Ruth's case, it may be a test of your character that might open up new doors of opportunity. God wants us to do our best, even with the small and seemingly insignificant tasks.

17   L E S S O N   2

16. *What prevents people from consistently doing their best work?*

17. *How do you react when you are given a task that does not require your full potential?*

18. *How can you emulate Ruth's attitude in your work?*

Read 1 Corinthians 4:12-13.

> *Paul's hard work did not bring him rewards. In fact, people cursed, slandered, and persecuted him for the work he was doing. When we work for God, our work may not receive recognition or adulation from others. But, like Paul, we can be confident that God will reward us for honoring him.*

19. *What rewards did Paul receive for his hard work?*

20. *In light of Paul's example, how should we respond when people criticize us for our work ethic?*

21. *How does Paul's experience change your perspective about your own work?*

Read 1 Timothy 6:17.

> *Paul told Timothy to warn the wealthy Christians in Ephesus about the uncertainty of wealth. This same warning is relevant for us. Those who have well-paying jobs must be careful not to put their hope in money instead of in the living God for their security. Companies downsize*

LESSON 2   18

and money depreciates, but God never changes. Do not depend on your company or your wealth to make you happy—God is the only one you can depend on!

22. In what ways do we depend on our work for fulfillment and security?

23. What happens when people focus too much of their time and attention on their work?

24. How can we guard against getting too wrapped up in our careers?

Read James 1:2-11.

Christians who do not have prestigious jobs or impressive careers should not be sad because they are great in the Lord's eyes. Some careers are not honored by the world. But Christians do not have to worry about that. We can find true contentment by developing our spiritual life, not by seeking status, position, or power in the workplace.

25. If you were demoted to the lowest position in your company, how do you think you would react?

26. Why do you think many people base their self-worth on their position, title, or status at work? Why is this dangerous?

27. If status, power, and wealth mean nothing to God, why do believers often show honor to people who possess them?

LESSON THREE

Life Begins on Friday

Some people *live* for the weekend! Correctly seeing the futility of dashing about for success, they put in the least amount of effort to get by, hurting both themselves and those who depend on them. In contrast, workaholics are consumed by work! They do not have time for weekends. Both extremes are foolish and irresponsible. Scripture encourages us to find the balance between laziness and busyness. This lesson will teach you the importance of being a diligent worker but also of knowing your limits.

◆◆◆◆◆ *STARTER*

1. *What is your favorite day of the week? Why?*

2. *When have you experienced bitter consequences for either working too hard or not working hard enough?*

LESSON 3   20

◆◆◆◆◆◆◆ *STUDY*

Read the following three sets of Bible passages and application notes.
Answer the questions for each set before moving on to the next.

Proverbs 13:4; 18:9; 21:25

KJV	NIV	NLT
The soul of the sluggard desireth, and hath nothing: but the soul of the diligent shall be made fat. . . . He also that is slothful in his work is brother to him that is a great waster. . . . The desire of the slothful killeth him; for his hands refuse to labour.	The sluggard craves and gets nothing, but the desires of the diligent are fully satisfied. . . . One who is slack in his work is brother to one who destroys. . . . The sluggard's craving will be the death of him, because his hands refuse to work.	Lazy people want much but get little, but those who work hard will prosper and be satisfied. . . . A lazy person is as bad as someone who destroys things. . . . The desires of lazy people will be their ruin, for their hands refuse to work.

Every day has twenty-four hours filled with opportunities to work, serve, and be productive. Yet it is so easy to waste time, letting life slip from our grasp. The book of Proverbs makes it clear that diligence—working hard and doing your best at any job given you—is a vital part of wise living. People who are diligent make good use of their time and resources, while those who are lazy waste them. Diligent people want to do high-quality work; lazy people are satisfied with the minimum standard. Determine to seize your opportunities to work diligently for God.

3. *Why do you think Scripture compares a lazy person to one who destroys?*

4. *Would your boss and coworkers describe you more as a hard worker or someone who tends to take it easy?*

LESSON 3

5. *What message do we send to others when we do sloppy work?*

6. *How would you like to improve your reputation at work?*

---

2 Thessalonians 3:6-8

KJV

Now we command you, brethren, in the name of our Lord Jesus Christ, that ye withdraw yourselves from every brother that walketh disorderly, and not after the tradition which he received of us. For yourselves know how ye ought to follow us: for we behaved not ourselves disorderly among you; Neither did we eat any man's bread for nought.

NIV

In the name of the Lord Jesus Christ, we command you, brothers, to keep away from every brother who is idle and does not live according to the teaching you received from us. For you yourselves know how you ought to follow our example. We were not idle when we were with you, nor did we eat anyone's food without paying for it.

NLT

And now, dear brothers and sisters, we give you this command with the authority of our Lord Jesus Christ: Stay away from any Christian who lives in idleness and doesn't follow the tradition of hard work we gave you. For you know that you ought to follow our example. We were never lazy when we were with you. We never accepted food from anyone without paying for it.

Paul and his companions worked hard, buying what they needed rather than becoming a burden to any of the believers. Paul did not tell the Thessalonians to work themselves to the bone but to work hard enough to provide for themselves. There is a difference between leisure and laziness. Relaxation and recreation provide a necessary and much-needed balance to our lives, but when it is time to work, we should jump right in. Do not make excuses to get out of doing your work or try to rationalize your laziness. Take your responsibilities seriously and do your part.

LESSON 3

7. Why do you think Paul gives such a harsh warning to stay away from idle people?

8. How does spending time with a lazy, unmotivated person affect your work?

9. What good or bad work habits have you picked up from your friends or coworkers?

10. How do you think the people around you are affected by your work habits?

Galatians 6:4-5

KJV
But let every man prove his own work, and then shall he have rejoicing in himself alone, and not in another. For every man shall bear his own burden.

NIV
Each one should test his own actions. Then he can take pride in himself, without comparing himself to somebody else, for each one should carry his own load.

NLT
Be sure to do what you should, for then you will enjoy the personal satisfaction of having done your work well, and you won't need to compare yourself to anyone else. For we are each responsible for our own conduct.

23 LESSON 3

Paul says there is no need to compare ourselves to others. God wants you to do the work he has given to you. Worrying about what others think of you or how much they have accomplished will only use up valuable time and energy. Instead, focus on your own responsibilities, use your time wisely, and know your limits. Work hard, go above and beyond when needed, but do not become consumed by your work. Scripture warns against idleness, but going to the other extreme and overworking is neither wise nor healthy.

11. *Why do we tend to compare ourselves and our work to others?*

12. *Are you more prone to be busy or lazy?*

13. *What limits do you need to set for yourself so that your job will not consume too much of your life?*

14. *How can you use your time, talents, and resources at work more wisely?*

◆◆◆◆◆◆ *SUMMARY*

If you often need help getting motivated or completing your work, Scripture admonishes you to be diligent. If you are naturally hardworking, you may need to concentrate on setting realistic limits for yourself. Scripture encourages each person to "carry his own load." Whatever your job, God wants you to work to the best of your ability—not more, not less!

LESSON 3 24

15. *What is the single most important change you can make in your work habits this week?*

◆◆◆◆◆◆ SUPPLEMENTAL QUESTIONS

Read Genesis 31:38-42.

> *Jacob made it a habit to do more than what was expected of him. He worked hard even after several pay cuts. His diligence eventually paid off, and he saw the rewards of his efforts. Hard work pleases God, earns recognition and advancement, enhances your reputation, builds others' confidence in you, gives you experience and knowledge, and develops your spiritual maturity. Instead of giving in to the temptation of laziness, make a habit of doing more than what is expected of you.*

16. *When have you experienced the rewards of diligence?*

17. *In what circumstances are you most tempted to slack off in your work?*

18. *In what area of your job can you easily do more than what is expected of you?*

Read Genesis 39:21-23.

> *As a prisoner and slave, Joseph could have seen his work as useless. Instead, he did his best with each small task given to him. His diligence and positive attitude were noticed by the warden, who promoted Joseph to prison administrator. Follow Joseph's example by doing your best to accomplish each small task you encounter at work. Faithful completion of mundane tasks is a great accomplishment. Remember how God turned Joseph's situation around. God will notice your efforts and reward your faithfulness to him.*

25   L E S S O N   3

19. *What small or menial tasks at work do you dread?*

20. *How does Joseph's example inspire you to change your attitude about that aspect of your job?*

Read Numbers 32:16-19.

> The land on the east side of the Jordan had been conquered. The hard work had been done by all the tribes together. But the tribes of Reuben and Gad and the half-tribe of Manasseh did not stop working after their land had been secured. They promised to keep working with the others until everyone had their portion of the land. They did not quit early because they had what they wanted. And neither should we.

21. *What are some examples of pressures or factors that keep us from helping others at work?*

22. *Do you usually look for excuses to escape extra work, or do you regularly go out of your way to help your coworkers?*

23. *In what small, practical way can you help a particular coworker this next week?*

Read Proverbs 6:6-11.

> Those last few moments of sleep are delicious—we savor them as we resist beginning another workday. But Proverbs warns against giving in to the temptation of laziness, of sleeping instead of working. The ant is used as an example because it utilizes its energy and

LESSON 3

resources economically. If laziness drives us to take a break now, necessity may soon bar us from the legitimate rest we should enjoy.

24. When have you suffered the consequences of laziness?

25. Whom do you admire as a hard worker?

26. What practical lessons can you learn from that person's example and apply to your own work?

Read 2 Thessalonians 3:11-13.

Some people in the early church believed that because Christ would return any day, people should set aside their responsibilities, quit work, do no future planning, and just wait for the Lord. But their inactivity only led them into sin. An idle person who does not find useful work ends up filling his or her time with less than helpful activities. We are not to live irresponsibly—using Christ's tarrying as an excuse not to work. We must keep on working until the end of our life or until the return of our Savior.

27. How should the hope of Christ's return affect our work?

28. How can we work in a way that shows our readiness for Christ's return?

29. In what ways can you use your time and talents more responsibly at work this week?

LESSON FOUR

You Deserve a Break

Faster cars, bigger houses, exotic vacations, designer clothes—many people think that if they work harder, they can have it all! But Scripture warns against working hard just to get rich or become successful. If we try to measure up to society's standards for fame and success, we may neglect our true purpose—to please God and honor him in all we do. Yes, we need to work for a living, but God also wants us to rest from work, trusting him to supply all our needs. This lesson will encourage you to maintain a healthy balance between work and rest.

◆◆◆◆◆ *STARTER*

1. *What time of year do you most need a vacation? Why?*

2. *What would you do with an extra day off every week?*

LESSON 4

STUDY

Read the following three sets of Bible passages and application notes. Answer the questions for each set before moving on to the next.

Exodus 20:8-11

KJV

Remember the sabbath day, to keep it holy. Six days shalt thou labour, and do all thy work: But the seventh day is the sabbath of the LORD thy God: in it thou shalt not do any work, thou, nor thy son, nor thy daughter, thy manservant, nor thy maidservant, nor thy cattle, nor thy stranger that is within thy gates: For in six days the LORD made heaven and earth, the sea, and all that in them is, and rested the seventh day: wherefore the LORD blessed the sabbath day, and hallowed it.

NIV

Remember the Sabbath day by keeping it holy. Six days you shall labor and do all your work, but the seventh day is a Sabbath to the LORD your God. On it you shall not do any work, neither you, nor your son or daughter, nor your manservant or maidservant, nor your animals, nor the alien within your gates. For in six days the LORD made the heavens and the earth, the sea, and all that is in them, but he rested on the seventh day. Therefore the LORD blessed the Sabbath day and made it holy.

NLT

Remember to observe the Sabbath day by keeping it holy. Six days a week are set apart for your daily duties and regular work, but the seventh day is a day of rest dedicated to the LORD your God. On that day no one in your household may do any kind of work. This includes you, your sons and daughters, your male and female servants, your livestock, and any foreigners living among you. For in six days the LORD made the heavens, the earth, the sea, and everything in them; then he rested on the seventh day. That is why the LORD blessed the Sabbath day and set it apart as holy.

After God created the world, he rested from his work. It should not amaze us that he also wants us to rest! Without time off from work, life loses its meaning. In our day—as in Moses'—taking time off is not easy. We live in a fast-paced world! There always seems to be more work to do, and we can sometimes feel guilty for stopping at all. But God tells us that rest is appropriate and right. Without a Sabbath we will forget the purpose for all of our activity and end up working for the wrong reasons.

LESSON 4

3. *What was your attitude toward the Sabbath before you started this study?*

4. *How do people rationalize or excuse their failure to observe a day of rest from work?*

5. *How do you feel on Monday mornings when you have spent the entire weekend working?*

6. *In what specific ways do you need to change the way you spend your time off from work?*

Proverbs 23:4-5

KJV	NIV	NLT
Labour not to be rich: cease from thine own wisdom. Wilt thou set thine eyes upon that which is not? for riches certainly make themselves wings; they fly away as an eagle toward heaven.	Do not wear yourself out to get rich; have the wisdom to show restraint. Cast but a glance at riches, and they are gone, for they will surely sprout wings and fly off to the sky like an eagle.	Don't weary yourself trying to get rich. Why waste your time? For riches can disappear as though they had the wings of a bird!

LESSON 4

Some people totally give themselves to the pursuit of self-gratification and personal advancement. They are willing to do whatever it takes to get the next raise or promotion. They hope their hard work will bring them money, power, success, and happiness. But they are inevitably disappointed. Proverbs warns us against working hard to get rich or to achieve power, because these things never lead to true contentment. If you want to please God, work for him, not yourself, and observe a regular time of rest and worship to keep your ambition and goals under God's control.

7. *Why do you think so many people wear themselves out to get rich?*

8. *In practical terms, what does it mean to work for God instead of ourselves?*

9. *How can you determine whether your motives for working are pure?*

10. *What does a willingness to rest from work reveal about a person's priorities and goals?*

LESSON 4

Psalm 127:1-2

KJV	NIV	NLT
Except the LORD build the house, they labour in vain that build it: except the LORD keep the city, the watchman waketh but in vain. It is vain for you to rise up early, to sit up late, to eat the bread of sorrows: for so he giveth his beloved sleep.	Unless the LORD builds the house, its builders labor in vain. Unless the LORD watches over the city, the watchmen stand guard in vain. In vain you rise early and stay up late, toiling for food to eat— for he grants sleep to those he loves.	Unless the LORD builds a house, the work of the builders is useless. Unless the LORD protects a city, guarding it with sentries will do no good. It is useless for you to work so hard from early morning until late at night, anxiously working for food to eat; for God gives rest to his loved ones.

God is not against human effort. Hard work honors God. But working to the exclusion of rest may be a cover-up for doubts that God will provide for our needs. Scripture promises that God grants sleep to those he loves. People who trust God do not have trouble taking time off from work. They work to please God and rest to please God. But people who are working for themselves rise early, stay up late, and work their fingers to the bone striving to achieve their goals. And when they are not working, they are usually worrying about it. Examine your willingness to rest from work. You may discover for whom you are really working.

11. *What do you usually think about as you drift off to sleep at night?*

12. *How can the wrong motives for working rob us of God's blessings?*

13. *Why is it so difficult to trust God with our needs?*

LESSON 4   32

14. *In what area or aspect of your job do you need to trust God more? How can you do that?*

◆◆◆◆◆◆◆ SUMMARY

Working for God is important, but so is taking a break from work to focus our attention on him. All of life's work must have God as the foundation, otherwise it is ultimately senseless. Do not make the mistake of leaving God out of your work—if you do, all your accomplishments will be wasted. Make serving God your highest priority, focus on him during your times of rest, and let him work through you on the job. When you work for God, he will help you enjoy both your times of work and your times of rest.

15. *What specific changes can you make in your weekly routine to establish a better balance of work and rest?*

◆◆◆◆◆◆◆ SUPPLEMENTAL QUESTIONS

Read Joshua 4:1-24.

> *After the Israelites crossed the Jordan River, God directed them to take time to build a memorial. This focused their attention on God and reminded them that he was guiding them into the Promised Land. As we are busy doing our work, we need to set aside quiet moments to focus our attention on God.*

16. *What kind of memorials should Christians build today?*

17. *How can you stay focused on God, even during busy times at work?*

18. When can you set aside a quiet time from your work this week to spend with God?

Read Mark 6:31.

> Jesus took his disciples away from their work to rest. Working hard is important, but Jesus recognized that to work effectively, people need periods of rest and renewal. Hard work honors God, but working to the exclusion of rest displeases him. We should acknowledge and appreciate God's gift of rest and refreshment. Take time to enjoy the other gifts God has given and realize that it is God who gives out the assignments and rewards, not us.

19. Why do you think some people refuse to rest from their work?

20. When could you take a personally refreshing break from your work this week?

21. How can you make the best use of that time of refreshment?

Read 1 Timothy 6:6-10.

> Many people work endlessly to get more money because they believe that money will make them happy. But this is not God's purpose for work. As Christians, we should strive to honor God in our work, not merely strive to get rich. Loving God and others sums up the Ten Commandments. But the love of money is a root of all kinds of evil. That is why God tells us to be content with what we have.

22. On a scale of one to ten, how important is your job to you?

LESSON 4

23. *How can we determine whether we depend too much on our jobs for security and fulfillment?*

24. *How can you guard against placing too much importance on your work?*

Read Ephesians 4:28.

Paul encouraged those who had previously earned a living dishonestly to find an honest job doing something useful so that they could share with the needy. Our goal should not be to gain wealth, fame, or the admiration of others (although that may happen) but to honor God with our work. God is honored when we do our work well, help and encourage those who work alongside us, and give generously of the money we earn to help those in need.

25. *What do you think motivates your coworkers to come to work each day?*

26. *How do these motives compare to what Paul says our goal should be in working?*

27. *Who is one needy person you can help in some way this week with some of the money you earn from your work?*

LESSON FIVE

You Cannot Do It All

If work was your only responsibility, life would be easy! But in addition to your role as employer or employee, you have many other roles: spouse, neighbor, friend, volunteer, parent, teacher, coach, and the list goes on. In those rare moments when you are holding it all together and everyone is happy, you feel exhausted. But if you neglect one area, your friends or loved ones can be disappointed and leave you feeling guilty. Fortunately, Scripture offers help. This lesson will show you how to balance the demands of your work with all of your other responsibilities. You will learn that you can't do it *all*, but with God's help, you can do what is most important.

◆◆◆◆◆ STARTER

1. *How do you usually greet your family when you get home from work?*

2. *List all your major responsibilities. How many are you juggling?*

LESSON 5

········ ***STUDY***

Read the following three sets of Bible passages and application notes. Answer the questions for each set before moving on to the next.

Proverbs 31:10, 14-16, 26-28

KJV

Who can find a virtuous woman? for her price is far above rubies. . . . She is like the merchants' ships; she bringeth her food from afar. She riseth also while it is yet night, and giveth meat to her household, and a portion to her maidens. She considereth a field, and buyeth it: with the fruit of her hands she planteth a vineyard. . . . She openeth her mouth with wisdom; and in her tongue is the law of kindness. She looketh well to the ways of her household, and eateth not the bread of idleness. Her children arise up, and call her blessed; her husband also, and he praiseth her.

NIV

A wife of noble character who can find? She is worth far more than rubies. . . . She is like the merchant ships, bringing her food from afar. She gets up while it is still dark; she provides food for her family and portions for her servant girls. She considers a field and buys it; out of her earnings she plants a vineyard. . . . She speaks with wisdom, and faithful instruction is on her tongue. She watches over the affairs of her household and does not eat the bread of idleness. Her children arise and call her blessed; her husband also, and he praises her.

NLT

Who can find a virtuous and capable wife? She is worth more than precious rubies. . . . She is like a merchant's ship; she brings her food from afar. She gets up before dawn to prepare breakfast for her household and plan the day's work for her servant girls. She goes out to inspect a field and buys it; with her earnings she plants a vineyard. . . . When she speaks, her words are wise, and kindness is the rule when she gives instructions. She carefully watches all that goes on in her household and does not have to bear the consequences of laziness. Her children stand and bless her. Her husband praises her.

The woman described in this passage balances the demands of work and family beautifully! In addition to being an excellent wife and mother, she is also a manufacturer, importer, manager, realtor, farmer, seamstress, and merchant. She knows that her work is important and worthwhile, so she uses her time wisely and works hard. She also finds time to help her husband, instruct her children, and minister to the needy. This portrait of the ideal woman is designed to encourage us to work hard and care for our families. But we should not feel we have to imitate every detail of this woman's life. We cannot be just like her, but we can learn from her resourcefulness, industry, discipline, and wisdom.

3. When have you felt intimidated by the example of someone who seems to have it all together?

4. What are the values and priorities of the woman described in this passage?

5. What can you learn from her example about managing time?

6. How can you apply one principle from this passage to help you balance your work and family obligations?

LESSON 5

Ecclesiastes 3:1, 9-11

KJV

To every thing there is a season, and a time to every purpose under the heaven: . . . What profit hath he that worketh in that wherein he laboureth? I have seen the travail, which God hath given to the sons of men to be exercised in it. He hath made every thing beautiful in his time: also he hath set the world in their heart, so that no man can find out the work that God maketh from the beginning to the end.

NIV

There is a time for everything, and a season for every activity under heaven: . . . What does the worker gain from his toil? I have seen the burden God has laid on men. He has made everything beautiful in its time. He has also set eternity in the hearts of men.

NLT

There is a time for everything, a season for every activity under heaven. . . . What do people really get for all their hard work? I have thought about this in connection with the various kinds of work God has given people to do. God has made everything beautiful for its own time. He has planted eternity in the human heart.

The writer of Ecclesiastes encourages us to discover, accept, and appreciate God's perfect timing! God gives us different work and family demands at different stages of life. Sometimes we have to put in extra hours at work and postpone a family outing or miss a social event. At other times, we have to choose low-stress jobs or reduced hours to devote more time to dealing with personal or family problems. Some jobs require sixty hours a week or have revolving or unpredictable schedules, and people have to decide whether those jobs are worth the corresponding sacrifices. Whatever your work situation, remember that timing is important! Carefully choose your priorities, keeping in mind that everything is beautiful in its time.

7. *Why do you think we put so much pressure on ourselves to do everything all at once?*

8. *How can we relieve some of the unnecessary pressures of work and life?*

LESSON 5

9. How would you describe the major challenges of balancing work and family that you face at this stage in your life?

10. What help or encouragement have you gained from this passage to handle those challenges?

James 1:5-6

KJV	NIV	NLT
If any of you lack wisdom, let him ask of God, that giveth to all men liberally, and upbraideth not; and it shall be given him. But let him ask in faith, nothing wavering. For he that wavereth is like a wave of the sea driven with the wind and tossed.	If any of you lacks wisdom, he should ask God, who gives generously to all without finding fault, and it will be given to him. But when he asks, he must believe and not doubt, because he who doubts is like a wave of the sea, blown and tossed by the wind.	If you need wisdom— if you want to know what God wants you to do— ask him, and he will gladly tell you. He will not resent your asking. But when you ask him, be sure that you really expect him to answer, for a doubtful mind is as unsettled as a wave of the sea that is driven and tossed by the wind.

No matter how long you have been married, or how many children you have at home, or how many years you have been at the same job, the stage you are in now has its own unique challenges! In every cycle of life, we need God's help to know what we should be doing and how to balance the conflicting demands of work and family. James simply advises us to ask God for wisdom. Whenever you need help making a decision or you face a problem at home or at work, pray to God, and he will give you the wisdom you need.

11. How do you typically respond when your work interferes with your responsibilities at home?

LESSON 5   40

12. *How do problems at work affect your family time?*

13. *Why do you think we sometimes neglect to pray about work-related problems?*

14. *For what specific problem or challenge in your work or home do you need wisdom from God?*

◆◆◆◆◆◆ SUMMARY

No matter how much the world tries to convince us we can do it all, we simply cannot! Trying to live up to unrealistic expectations will only result in frustration, anger, and guilt. We need to recognize our limits and choose our priorities for each stage of life. We can do what is necessary now and wait to work on the rest of our goals and dreams later. Most important, we need to ask God to help us choose our priorities and give us the wisdom we so desperately need.

15. *When can you take some time this week to evaluate your work responsibilities and family needs and devise a plan to better manage both areas of obligation?*

41 LESSON 5

◆◆◆◆◆ *SUPPLEMENTAL QUESTIONS*

Read Deuteronomy 6:1-9.

Parents are responsible to teach their children how to love and obey God. The best way to do this is to weave religious education into the fabric of their daily lives. Your work schedule may not allow you to have regular family devotions, but you can teach your children about God as you drive them to soccer practice or tuck them into bed at night. Take your responsibility to teach your children about God seriously. No matter how demanding your job is, make time to train your children in the ways of the Lord.

16. *How did the Israelites balance the demands of work with their responsibility to teach their children about God?*

17. *In what creative ways can we teach our children about God, even when we are burdened with busy work schedules?*

18. *How can you keep your work from interfering with the spiritual training of your children?*

Read 1 Kings 1:6.

David worked hard for God as the king of Israel, but as a parent he often failed both God and his children. Moral and spiritual character take years to build and require constant attention and patient discipline. Christians cannot take for granted the spiritual well-being of their children. The Bible tells us to provide for the physical needs of our families but not to neglect their spiritual and emotional needs. We should never use our jobs as an excuse to compromise the spiritual well-being of our families.

19. *In what ways do you think David's work interfered with his ability or desire to be a good parent?*

LESSON 5   42

20. *How does your work impact your parenting?*

21. *How can you guard against taking the spiritual development of your children for granted?*

Read Ecclesiastes 9:7-9.

The writer of Ecclesiastes advised married people to appreciate and enjoy the companionship God had given them. How sad it is when people get caught up in today's rat race and become so consumed with work that they neglect their spouses and families. The future is so uncertain. We should enjoy God's gifts while we are able to do so. Do not let your work take up so much of your time and energy that you have nothing left to give to the people you love the most.

22. *What attitudes do people in your workplace have about marriage?*

23. *How does the viewpoint in this passage compare to the attitude of your coworkers?*

24. *What is one way you can use your time at work more wisely so that your job does not interfere with your family time?*

Read Psalm 127:3-5.

This psalm reminds us of God's view of children: They are a heritage from the Lord and a reward. No matter how demanding our jobs are or how desperately we want to move up the corporate ladder, we should not work to the neglect of our children. We may have to turn down a promotion or sacrifice some of the perks of the job to spend time with our children. But whatever we give up, it is worth it when we consider how important children are in God's sight.

43 LESSON 5

25. *On a scale of one to ten, how willing are you to make job-related sacrifices for the benefit of your children?*

26. *How can we communicate to our children that they are more valuable to us than our jobs?*

27. *How do you need to change the way you work to better communicate your love to your family?*

Read 1 Timothy 5:8.

Paul tells us that those who do not provide for their relatives are worse than unbelievers. Providing for our family is a serious, God-given responsibility. It involves much more than financial provision. God wants us to provide for the physical, emotional, and spiritual needs of our families. Work to clothe, feed, and shelter your family, but make time to care for its emotional and spiritual needs too.

28. *Why is the neglect of family responsibilities such a serious offense?*

29. *What happens when Christians fail to provide for their family members?*

30. *How does this verse change your attitude toward your responsibilities at work and at home?*

LESSON SIX

If It Were Not for My Boss

Not many of us enjoy being told what to do. We naturally prefer to do our work our own way. This natural human tendency to resist authority can cause problems at work. No matter who we work for, the Bible tells us to respect and obey those in authority over us. Acknowledging Jesus Christ as the true Master motivates us to do our best work, even though your boss may be less than perfect. This lesson will encourage you to show respect for your employer and work to the best of your ability because you are ultimately serving Jesus Christ.

STARTER

1. *Who was the worst boss you have ever had? Why?*

2. *How would you describe the ideal boss?*

LESSON 6   46

◆◆◆◆◆◆ *STUDY*

Read the following three sets of Bible passages and application notes. Answer the questions for each set before moving on to the next.

Ephesians 6:5-9

KJV

Servants, be obedient to them that are your masters according to the flesh, with fear and trembling, in singleness of your heart, as unto Christ; Not with eyeservice, as menpleasers; but as the servants of Christ, doing the will of God from the heart; With good will doing service, as to the Lord, and not to men: Knowing that whatsoever good thing any man doeth, the same shall he receive of the Lord, whether he be bond or free. And, ye masters, do the same things unto them, forbearing threatening: knowing that your Master also is in heaven; neither is there respect of persons with him.

NIV

Slaves, obey your earthly masters with respect and fear, and with sincerity of heart, just as you would obey Christ. Obey them not only to win their favor when their eye is on you, but like slaves of Christ, doing the will of God from your heart. Serve wholeheartedly, as if you were serving the Lord, not men, because you know that the Lord will reward everyone for whatever good he does, whether he is slave or free. And masters, treat your slaves in the same way. Do not threaten them, since you know that he who is both their Master and yours is in heaven, and there is no favoritism with him.

NLT

Slaves, obey your earthly masters with deep respect and fear. Serve them sincerely as you would serve Christ. Work hard, but not just to please your masters when they are watching. As slaves of Christ, do the will of God with all your heart. Work with enthusiasm, as though you were working for the Lord rather than for people. Remember that the Lord will reward each one of us for the good we do, whether we are slaves or free. And in the same way, you masters must treat your slaves right. Don't threaten them; remember, you both have the same Master in heaven, and he has no favorites.

Paul's instructions encourage responsibility and integrity on the job. Christian employees should do their jobs to the best of their ability, as if Jesus were their supervisor. They should work hard all the time, not just when the boss is watching. And Christian employers should treat their employees fairly and with respect. Remember that no matter whom you work for, and no matter who works for you, the one you ultimately should want to please is your Father in heaven. Though your boss may not notice your good work, you will surely receive your reward from the true Master.

47   LESSON 6

3. *What impure motives does this passage warn us to guard against?*

4. *How do you work differently when your boss is around compared to when he or she is not watching?*

5. *When has your hard work gone unnoticed? How did you feel?*

6. *How do you think the quality of your work would change if Jesus sat beside you at work every day?*

LESSON 6

Colossians 3:22-24

KJV	NIV	NLT
Servants, obey in all things your masters according to the flesh; not with eyeservice, as menpleasers; but in singleness of heart, fearing God: And whatsoever ye do, do it heartily, as to the Lord, and not unto men; Knowing that of the Lord ye shall receive the reward of the inheritance: for ye serve the Lord Christ.	Slaves, obey your earthly masters in everything; and do it, not only when their eye is on you and to win their favor, but with sincerity of heart and reverence for the Lord. Whatever you do, work at it with all your heart, as working for the Lord, not for men, since you know that you will receive an inheritance from the Lord as a reward. It is the Lord Christ you are serving.	You slaves must obey your earthly masters in everything you do. Try to please them all the time, not just when they are watching you. Obey them willingly because of your reverent fear of the Lord. Work hard and cheerfully at whatever you do, as though you were working for the Lord rather than for people. Remember that the Lord will give you an inheritance as your reward, and the Master you are serving is Christ.

Paul is not condoning slavery in this passage; he is encouraging Christians to work wholeheartedly and do their best all the time. Even if we feel trapped in our jobs, we are still serving Christ. Even if our tasks seem insignificant or menial, we should work as though Jesus were watching us. God will reward good workers and will punish those who misuse their talents or do only the bare minimum required of them. Ultimately, we are all serving Christ, no matter what job we happen to have right now.

7. *Why do you think these were important instructions for the early church?*

8. *What will help to remind you that you are working for Jesus and not yourself?*

9. *To what degree did you work with all you heart this week?*

49　　　　　　　　　　　　　　　　　　　　L E S S O N　6

10. *How could you put more of your heart into your work this week?*

Hebrews 12:1-3

KJV
Wherefore seeing we also are compassed about with so great a cloud of witnesses, let us lay aside every weight, and the sin which doth so easily beset us, and let us run with patience the race that is set before us, Looking unto Jesus the author and finisher of our faith; who for the joy that was set before him endured the cross, despising the shame, and is set down at the right hand of the throne of God. For consider him that endured such contradiction of sinners against himself, lest ye be wearied and faint in your minds.

NIV
Therefore, since we are surrounded by such a great cloud of witnesses, let us throw off everything that hinders and the sin that so easily entangles, and let us run with perseverance the race marked out for us. Let us fix our eyes on Jesus, the author and perfecter of our faith, who for the joy set before him endured the cross, scorning its shame, and sat down at the right hand of the throne of God. Consider him who endured such opposition from sinful men, so that you will not grow weary and lose heart.

NLT
Therefore, since we are surrounded by such a huge crowd of witnesses to the life of faith, let us strip off every weight that slows us down, especially the sin that so easily hinders our progress. And let us run with endurance the race that God has set before us. We do this by keeping our eyes on Jesus, on whom our faith depends from start to finish. He was willing to die a shameful death on the cross because of the joy he knew would be his afterward. Now he is seated in the place of highest honor beside God's throne in heaven. Think about all he endured when sinful people did such terrible things to him, so that you don't become weary and give up.

Being a Christian in the workplace is not easy. When we focus on the shortcomings of the boss or other difficult aspects of the job, we will be tempted to give up. But focusing on Christ motivates us to keep working hard because he deserves our best effort. Other believers can

LESSON 6

also help you keep the proper perspective. You are not the only one with a demanding boss or overwhelming responsibilities at work. Other Christians face similar struggles. You can encourage one another to persevere.

11. *Why is it difficult to throw off everything that hinders and entangles us?*

12. *How can you fix your eyes on Jesus as you work this week?*

13. *How can other believers inspire us to work wholeheartedly for God?*

14. *Who can you turn to for help in dealing with the challenges and frustrations of your job?*

◆◆◆◆◆◆◆ SUMMARY

All three passages in this lesson remind us that Jesus Christ is our true Master. We work for *him*. Focusing on Christ will motivate you to work diligently and cheerfully, no matter who is giving you orders or watching you work. Your boss may not notice your efforts, but God promises to watch all you do.

51　　　　　　　　　　　　　　　　　　　L E S S O N　6

15. *Which person in authority over you most needs your prayer this week?*

♦♦♦♦♦ *SUPPLEMENTAL QUESTIONS*

Read Haggai 2:4.

> *Judah's people had returned to worshiping God, and God had promised to bless their efforts. But it was time for them to get to work. Knowing that God is with us should give us the desire and motivation to do what God has in mind for us. God has given you a job to do. Be strong and work hard because God is with you!*

16. *How do you think the people of Judah responded to this message from the Lord?*

17. *When have you lacked motivation to work?*

18. *How does the promise of God's presence affect your motivation to work?*

Read 1 Timothy 6:1-2.

> *Paul's counsel for the master and slave relationship in this passage can be applied to the employer and employee relationship today. Employees should work hard, showing respect for their employers. In turn, employers should be fair. Our relationships in the workplace should reflect our faithfulness to and love for Christ. Whatever kind of employer you work for, God wants you to treat him or her with respect. If Paul instructed slaves to work hard for their masters, we should give our best effort for our employers.*

LESSON 6

19. *In what practical ways can we show respect for our employers?*

20. *When the boss is not around, do you usually work enthusiastically and cheerfully, or do you complain?*

21. *How does this passage challenge you to change your attitude toward your boss?*

Read 1 Thessalonians 5:12-14.

> *Paul encouraged the Thessalonians to respect those who were in authority over them. Just as we show respect for church leaders, we should also respect those over us in the workplace. How can you show respect to the people for whom you work? Express your appreciation, tell them how you have been helped by their leadership, and let them know that you want to support them. If you say nothing, how will they know where you stand?*

22. *What often keeps us from honestly expressing our feelings or ideas to those in authority over us?*

23. *What have you done in the past to demonstrate respect and appreciation for your boss?*

24. *How can you do a better job of supporting your boss in the future?*

If you enjoyed this topical study, be sure to check out the other seven studies on:

Character
Friendship
Money
Parenting
Priorities
Stress
Worship

If your group completes one or more of the studies listed above and wants to study a book of the Bible for a change of pace, consider using one of the Life Application Bible Studies listed below. These guides help you study a book of the Bible using an application-oriented format.

Genesis TLB
Joshua TLB
Judges NIV
Ruth & Esther TLB
1 Samuel NIV
Ezra & Nehemiah NIV
Proverbs NIV
Daniel NIV
Matthew NIV
Mark NIV & TLB
Luke NIV
John NIV
Acts NIV & TLB
Romans NIV
1 Corinthians NIV
2 Corinthians NIV
Galatians & Ephesians NIV
Philippians & Colossians NIV
1 & 2 Thessalonians & Philemon NIV
1 & 2 Timothy & Titus NIV
Hebrews NIV
James NIV
1 & 2 Peter & Jude NIV
1, 2, & 3 John NIV
Revelation NIV